W9-ALJ-105

Soil

by Adele D. Richardson

Consultant:
Francesca Pozzi, Research Associate
Center for International Earth Science Information Network
Columbia University

Bridgestone Books
an imprint of Capstone Press
Mankato, Minnesota

Bridgestone Books are published by Capstone Press
151 Good Counsel Drive, P.O. Box 669, Mankato, Minnesota 56002
http://www.capstone-press.com

Library of Congress Cataloging-in-Publication Data
Richardson, Adele, 1966–
    Soil/by Adele D. Richardson.
    p. cm.—(The Bridgestone science library)
    Includes bibliographical references and index.
    ISBN 0-7368-0954-6
    1. Soils—Juvenile literature. [1. Soils.] I. Title. II. Series.
S591.3 R53 2002
631.4—dc21   00-012654

Summary: Discusses the different types of soil, its properties, erosion, pollution, and how
    humans can protect soil.

Editorial Credits
Erika Mikkelson, editor; Karen Risch, product planning editor; Linda Clavel, designer and
    illustrator; Jeff Anderson, photo researcher

Photo Credits
Digital Wisdom, globe images
Don and Pat Valenti/Root Resources, 10
Inga Spence/TOM STACK & ASSOCIATES, 18
International Stock/Bob Firth, 12
John Elk III, 4
Larry Ditto/KAC Productions, 6
Mary A. Root/Root Resources, 16
Robert Maust/Photo Agora, 20
Robert McCaw, 8
Visuals Unlimited/Wally Eberhart, cover, 1; Norris Blake, 14

Cover photo: Profile of soil in Crosby, Minnesota

1 2 3 4 5 6 07 06 05 04 03 02

Table of Contents

Fun Fact

Clumps of soil are called peds. Most peds measure less than 6 inches (15 centimeters) across.

What Is Soil?

Soil covers most land on Earth. Plants and trees grow in soil. Farmers also grow crops in soil.

Pieces of humus and rock make up soil. Humus is the remains of dead plants and animals. Plants and animals begin to rot when they die. Insects and other small animals break down the remains into the soil. Humus has many nutrients that help new plants grow.

Wind, water, and ice break rocks on Earth's surface into small pieces. Water, wind, and small animals mix these pieces with humus to form soil.

Soil is one of Earth's most important resources. Plants and trees need soil to live. People and animals depend on plants for food. Plants also turn the gas carbon dioxide into oxygen. People need oxygen to breathe.

Crops grow well in rich, healthy soil.

Types of Soil

Different soils are found in different climates around the world. Dead plants and animals decay faster in warm, wet areas. This soil is richer and deeper than in dry areas.

Soil can be many different colors. People often think of soil as black or brown. Soil also can be red, yellow, white, tan, or gray. The color of soil depends on the types of rock and the amount of humus in it.

Sandy soils do not have much humus. They do not soak up much rain. Sandy soils usually are lighter colors. Deserts have sandy soil.

Clay is made of tiny rock pieces, sand, and humus. Clay soaks up and holds a lot of water. Clay can be many colors such as white, gray, red, or brown. People make bricks out of clay.

Loam is a very rich soil. Sand, clay, and decayed plants and animals make up this soil. Farmers sometimes plant crops in loam.

Aloe vera plants grow in sandy soil.

Nutrients in Soil

All plants and trees need nutrients to grow strong and healthy. Most plants and trees get their nutrients from soil and water. They soak up nutrients through their roots. Nitrogen, phosphorus, and potassium are three important soil nutrients for plants and trees.

Nitrogen is a nutrient that helps plants grow leaves. Nitrogen is part of a plant's chlorophyll. This green pigment allows plants to produce food and to grow. Plants and trees in nitrogen-rich soil are greener and produce more leaves.

Plants and trees need phosphorus to grow seeds and flowers. Phosphorus also helps build strong roots. Plants and trees with a lot of phosphorus produce larger flowers.

Potassium helps plants and trees grow strong roots. Plants and trees need potassium to make chlorophyll. Potassium also helps protect plants and trees from diseases.

Plants with dark green leaves grow in nitrogen-rich soil.

Animals in Soil

Millions of animals live in soil. Thousands of earthworms, insects, and spiders can live in 1 cubic foot (0.03 cubic meter) of soil.

Earthworms are common in soil. They live 1 to 48 inches (2.5 to 120 centimeters) underground. They eat soil and rotting plant leaves. Earthworms leave droppings that are rich in nutrients. These nutrients help plants grow larger and healthier.

Ants, termites, and other insects also live underground. They loosen soil and create burrows. More water and air can reach plant roots in loose soil. Plants grow better when they receive more water and air.

Larger animals also dig underground and loosen soil. Shrews, moles, and mice dig to find food. They eat insects and worms. Woodchucks, chipmunks, and skunks sleep and raise their young in underground burrows.

Some earthworms live close to the surface of soil.

Fun Fact

Soil forms in layers
called horizons.

Plants in Soil

Plants and trees need soil to grow. Their roots soak up nutrients in the soil. The roots also help create new soil and prevent erosion.

Roots grow deeper into the soil as plants and trees grow. The growing roots loosen the soil much like burrowing animals do. Plants and trees then receive more water and air through the loosened soil.

Tree roots are strong. They can crack roads and sidewalks as they grow. The growing roots break rocks in the soil into smaller pieces. The smaller pieces mix with humus to create more soil.

Plant and tree roots act like anchors. They keep plants and trees firmly in the ground. Roots also help plants and trees stand upright.

Roots also help protect soil from erosion. Wind and rain can erode, or wear away, loose soil more easily. Tree and plant roots act like a net. Roots hold soil together and protect it.

People can see tree roots when soil erodes.

What Is a Pedologist?

Pedologists are scientists who study soil. They may study soil by looking at it and touching it. They sometimes even taste it. Pedologists might taste the soil to find out what nutrients make it up. They help farmers keep soil healthy for growing crops. They also discover how soils become polluted. Pedologists help find ways to prevent soil pollution.

Topsoil

Topsoil is the uppermost layer of the earth. Most topsoil is loam. Loam soaks up and stores water. Plants and trees need water to grow. They can grow only where there is topsoil. Topsoil is almost completely humus.

Topsoil forms very slowly. A 1-inch (2.5-centimeter) layer of topsoil may take more than 500 years to form.

Different places in the world have different types of topsoil. The richness of topsoil depends on the climate. In warm climates, topsoil often is deeper and has more nutrients. These areas receive a great deal of rain. Rain forests have thick, rich soil. The topsoil there can be more than 3 feet (1 meter) thick.

Hot, dry places such as deserts have little topsoil. Few plants grow in these areas. Wind often blows away the loose soil. Some deserts have a very thin layer of topsoil. Other deserts do not have topsoil at all.

Farmers can grow crops in sandy loam.

Soil Erosion

Unprotected topsoil can erode easily. Wind is one force that can damage topsoil. Topsoil blows away when no trees or plants protect it from the wind. Plants and trees cannot be planted in areas where topsoil has eroded.

Water also can erode soil. Rain loosens soil. Light rain soaks into soil where plants and tree roots need it. But soil cannot soak up all the water when a lot of rain falls. Heavy rains sometimes cause floods. Flood waters often move quickly and forcefully. They wash soil into rivers and ditches.

Animals that graze on grass can cause erosion. Cows and sheep may eat too much grass in one area. The topsoil is left unprotected if animals eat grass down to the ground. Wind and water then can erode the topsoil more easily. If the topsoil is gone, new grass cannot grow to replace the old grass.

Wind easily blows away unprotected soil.

Soil Pollution

Pollution can damage soil. It can destroy the nutrients in soil. Plants and trees then become weak and die. Animals that eat the plants can become sick and weak. Pollution also harms animals that live in soil.

Farmers sometimes pollute soil. They may use pesticides to kill insects that eat their crops. Pesticides can build up in the soil. Plants begin to soak up the pesticides. The plants then may die. The plants may produce food that is harmful to people and animals.

People can damage soil in other ways. They may spray weed killers on their lawns. These chemicals stop dandelions and other weeds from growing in the grass. But these chemicals also harm the soil. Soap, paint, oil, and gasoline also can pollute soil. People can kill plants and trees if they spill these materials.

Harmful chemicals sprayed on crops can damage soil.

Saving Soil

Farmers can save soil. Different crops use different nutrients in the soil. Planting a variety of crops helps replace used nutrients in soil. Farmers can add fertilizers to soil. Fertilizers add nutrients to soil and help crops grow. Livestock farmers can make sure their animals do not graze too long in one area.

People can plant trees to help save soil. In forests, trees can be planted near one another. Their roots hold the soil together. People can leave dead branches and leaves on the forest floor. They will rot and turn into humus. In flat areas, people can plant trees to block the wind. Then the wind will not blow away the topsoil.

Everyone can help save soil by not littering. Trash that is on the ground can harm soil, plants, and animals. Keeping soil healthy helps all life on Earth.

People plant trees to protect soil from erosion.

Hands On: Soil and Water

Plants grow better in dark, rich topsoil. This soil has many nutrients and soaks up water well. You can compare rich soil and sand.

What You Need

Two small, clear plastic cups
Potting soil
Sand
Water
Tablespoon

What You Do

1. Fill half of one cup with potting soil. Fill half of the other cup with sand. Pack the potting soil and sand tightly.
2. Place one tablespoon of water into each cup. What happens?

The dark, rich soil quickly soaks up the water. Sand soaks up the water more slowly. Plants grow better in dark, rich soil. Water can easily get to plants' roots in this soil.

Words to Know

climate (KLYE-mit)—the usual weather in a place
erosion (e-ROH-zhuhn)—the wearing away of land by water, ice, or wind
humus (HYOO-muhs)—a rich, nutrient-filled layer of soil
loam (LOHM)—rich soil that is made up of sand, clay, and decayed plants and animals
nutrient (NOO-tree-uhnt)—a substance needed by a living thing to stay healthy
pesticide (PESS-ti-side)—a chemical used to kill insects and other pests that eat crops
pollution (puh-LOO-shuhn)—harmful materials that damage the environment

Read More

Bocknek, Jonathon. *Science of Soil.* Living Science. Milwaukee: Gareth Stevens, 1999.

Flanagan, Alice K. *Soil.* Simply Science. Minneapolis: Compass Point Books, 2000.

Olien, Becky. *Erosion.* The Bridgestone Science Library. Mankato, Minn.: Bridgestone Books, 2002.

Snedden, Robert. *Rocks and Soil.* Science Projects. Austin, Texas: Raintree Steck-Vaughn, 1999.

Useful Addresses

American Geological Institute
AGI Education Department
4220 King Street
Alexandria, VA 22302

Geological Survey of Canada Earth Sciences Sector
601 Booth Street
Ottawa, ON K1A 0E8
Canada

Internet Sites

Earth Science Enterprise
http://kids.earth.nasa.gov
Field Museum: Underground Adventure
http://www.fmnh.org/ua/
Great Plant Escape Case #2—Soiled Again
http://www.urbanext.uiuc.edu/gpe/case2/case2.html

Index